NO MORE HOLDING BACK

STUDY GUIDE
SIX SESSIONS

Emboldening Women to Move
Past Barriers, See Their Worth,
and Serve God Everywhere

Kat Armstrong

W PUBLISHING GROUP

AN IMPRINT OF THOMAS NELSON

Published in Nashville, Tennessee, by W Publishing. W Publishing is a registered trademark of Thomas Nelson, Inc.

Scripture quotations marked csb® are taken from the Christian Standard Bible®, Copyright © 2017 by Holman Bible Publishers. Used by permission. Christian Standard Bible®, and CSB®, are federally registered trademarks of Holman Bible Publishers.

Scripture quotations marked esv are taken from the esv® Bible (The Holy Bible, English Standard Version®). Copyright © 2001 by Crossway, a publishing ministry of Good News Publishers. Used by permission. All rights reserved.

Scripture quotations marked nasb are taken from the New American Standard Bible®. Copyright © 1960, 1962, 1963, 1968, 1971, 1972, 1973, 1975, 1977, 1995 by The Lockman Foundation. Used by permission. (www.Lockman.org).

Scripture quotations marked net taken from the net Bible®. Copyright ©1996–2006 by Biblical Studies Press, L.L.C. http://netbible.com. All rights reserved.

Scripture quotations marked are taken from The Holy Bible, New International Version®, niv®. Copyright © 1973, 1978, 1984, 2011 by Biblica, Inc.® Used by permission of Zondervan. All rights reserved worldwide. www.Zondervan.com. The "niv" and "New International Version" are trademarks registered in the United States Patent and Trademark Office by Biblica, Inc.®

Scripture quotations marked nlt are taken from the Holy Bible, New Living Translation. © 1996, 2004, 2007, 2013, 2015 by Tyndale House Foundation. Used by permission of Tyndale House Publishers, Inc., Carol Stream, Illinois 60188. All rights reserved.

Scripture quotations marked tpt are from The Passion Translation®. Copyright © 2017, 2018 by Passion & Fire Ministries, Inc. Used by permission. All rights reserved. ThePassionTranslation.com.

ISBN: 978-0-310-098942.

Author's literary agent is Christopher Ferebee Agency.

CONTENTS

A MESSAGE FROM KAT

*E*verything changed when my friend Becky invited me to join her small group Bible study. At first I refused, citing the fact that people who "study" the Bible were strange. But, thankfully, she was persistent. She couldn't wait to share her friends and her Jesus with me.

Hesitant and suspicious, I finally surrendered after she showed up at my house unannounced to make the ask face-to-face. How could I refuse her? She'd made the ultimate sacrifice: fighting Houston traffic while driving across the city to pick me up. That's what Houstonians call true love.

Becky was right, of course. I needed the help of the group to learn how to love God and love others. Lessons I could only understand in the context of community. Because it was safe to ask questions and struggle with the mysteries of God.

I've often wondered what life would be like now had Becky not ushered me into a relationship with God and the community of faith. That's why I've been on my knees praying for you. Because I know firsthand the profound impact of opening your Bible to find the one true living God who's eager to embrace you.

Maybe it's been a long time since you've read the Scriptures. Maybe you are processing church hurt. Maybe somewhere along the way the passion you felt for God has morphed into caution or doubt. No matter where you are on your spiritual journey, God is waiting with open arms. Trust him this time. Trust him, again.

Love,

Kat Armstrong

HOW TO USE THIS GUIDE

Group Size

Even God is in community—with himself, as Father, Son, and Holy Spirit. That's why the *No More Holding Back* video curriculum was designed to be experienced while linking arms with other women. Ideally, your group will be four to six women but if your group is larger than six women, consider breaking into smaller groups for the discussion time. By including videos, notes, discussion questions, and personal study, this guide could be used in a home, at a church, or even over a quick meal before work or during your lunch break.

Resources

For this study you will need the *No More Holding Back* video or digital study and enough study guides for each person in your group. Each video is only 15 minutes long. Although it's not required, to enjoy the recommended reading in each session you also will need the *No More Holding Back* book.

Group Discussion

I struggle to find margin in my full schedule, even for the things that are the most important to me. That's why I think working through the material with a group could be the accountability we all need. Each session begins with a group discussion; you'll also notice time estimations throughout the material that indicate the length of time for each portion. I hope that helps you manage your time well while still leaving room for the Holy Spirit to direct your conversation. **Set aside approximately 60–90 minutes each time you gather your group.** Each part of the group time includes suggested time cues to keep your group on track and considerate of everyone's schedules. Check out *Loving Your Community Well* in the appendix for tips for great discussion time.

Personal Study

The personal study sections are meant to be completed between video and group session meetings. Each personal study section is intended to be approximately 45 minutes of total individual study time divided into three 15-minute segments. It's up to you if you want to work through the material one part at a time over the course of a few days or all in one sitting. Do what's best for your schedule and learning style. I didn't include any personal study homework for session 1, because I think your time would best be spent getting to know the other women in your group, even if you've been together for years. Those relationships are key.

Group Leaders

Taking the initiative to lead a group is sacred work that will be challenging *and* rewarding. I've been leading small groups for twenty years and I can say with confidence, you can do this. Why? Because *God* equips the people *he* calls by the power of *his* Spirit. The suggested time cues will help you keep your group time efficient and effective. Take a moment to read through the leader's guide in the back; it was designed to support you.

PART ONE

THE MESSAGES HOLDING WOMEN BACK

ONE

WHY ARE YOU EVEN HERE?

Group Time

Leader read Kat's message to group:

It's no accident that your attention is here for the moment. Cast aside those nagging fears that you won't give this study the time it deserves, and you should just quit while you're ahead. Reject the notion that this can wait. Because now is always the right time to reconnect with God. Plus, he's been patiently waiting to embrace you. Let his unconditional love override the normal apprehensions that accompany starting something new. Embrace this fresh start with gusto. God has carved out this space just for you.

With that in mind, welcome to Bible study!

Start with Prayer (2 minutes)

Before you launch, take a moment to start with group prayer. This would be a good time to invite the Holy Spirit to guide your group discussion and personal study time. The Bible teaches that there is one true living God who eternally exists in three persons: Father, Son, and Holy Spirit. And Jesus taught that the Holy Spirit is the Great Teacher (John 14) who would help us all reach our full potential. Since God has made a way for us to experience life-change through the Holy Spirit's power, go ahead and call on the Spirit in prayer. Ask God to teach everyone new things about himself through the Word of God.

Build Community (15 minutes)

You're in this together. So, use this time to go around the circle and have everyone introduce themselves and share why they wanted to be a part of this study by answering these questions:

- What brought you to this group?

- What do you hope to get out of this study?

Scripture Reading

Have one person read the following passage aloud:

MARK 12:28–34 NIV

One of the teachers of the law came and heard them debating. Noticing that Jesus had given them a good answer, he asked him, "Of all the commandments, which is the most important?"

"The most important one," answered Jesus, "is this: 'Hear, O Israel: The Lord our God, the Lord is one. Love the Lord your God with all your heart and with all your soul and with all your mind and with all your strength.' The second is this: 'Love your neighbor as yourself.' There is no commandment greater than these."

"Well said, teacher," the man replied. "You are right in saying that God is one and there is no other but him. To love him with all your heart, with all your understanding and with all your strength, and to love your neighbor as yourself is more important than all burnt offerings and sacrifices."

When Jesus saw that he had answered wisely, he said to him, "You are not far from the kingdom of God." And from then on no one dared ask him any more questions.

Watch Session 1 Video (15 minutes)

Video Notes

God did not design half of his priorities for women and the other half for men.

Some of the messages we hear in church hold women back from loving God with our all.

Group Discussion (25 minutes)

If your group is larger than six people, split up into smaller groups for discussion time.

1. Why do you think loving God with our hearts and souls is usually considered women's work and loving God with our minds and strength considered men's work?

2. According to the Mark passage read earlier, what are the two greatest priorities Jesus prescribes for the Christian life?

3. Who in your life lives out these priorities well? What is it about their life that reveals their priorities align with Jesus'?

4. In the video, the professor said, "Don't stop. Don't ever stop. Keep going sister of the faith." Who in your life encourages you to follow Christ? What do they say to you that is helpful?

5. What's the message holding you back from loving God with your all?

6. Metaphorically speaking, what would it look like to raise your hand more at church, school, at home, and/or work?

Ask God for Help (2 minutes)

While everyone in your group may have different reasons for joining this study, God is able to meet all of our needs: *"And my God will meet all your needs according to the riches of his glory in Christ Jesus"* (Philippians 4:19 NIV, italics added).

Take a moment to write a prayer to God asking him to accomplish the intentions you have for the group discussion and personal study time.

End in Prayer (2 minutes)

Before you end group time, take a few minutes to thank God for the Scriptures and the timeless truths they provide to us in any and every circumstance. Ask God to help each group member to be all-in for Jesus, holding nothing back from him.

Activity

This week you won't have any personal study material because I'm hoping you will meet with one person in your group and get to know her better. Maybe your group has been together for years and you are way past a first-name basis. Even so, taking this week and intentionally spending time one-on-one with a group member is your homework.

Preview

Leader read next week's preview to group:

Next time your group meets, we will address the obstacles many women face when they seek to apply the Scriptures to their lives. Messages like these: women are easily deceived, find their significance in marriage and motherhood, are too much to handle, and don't have a lot to offer God. We don't want to walk away from this study in a few weeks and just know more *about* the Great Commandment. We want to absorb God's truths and live them out! Before we can ask, "What does this Bible verse mean?" we have to ask ourselves if there is anything keeping us from absorbing the material in the first place.

Suggested Reading in
No More Holding Back:

Introduction: Why Are You Even Here?

STAY IN YOUR PLACE

Group Time

Leader read Kat's message to group:

I hope your one-on-one time served as another reminder that the God of the universe cares deeply about you and your sisters in the faith. Long before you decided to join this group, Jesus loved you.

This session will introduce you to a very common message holding women back: stay in your place. I still have lots of questions for God on the important role of women in society and the church, but I am absolutely certain that, as a woman, I am commanded by Jesus himself in the Great Commandment to pursue him. Which inevitably means we *can't* stay in our place. We have to move *toward* God.

Start with Prayer (2 minutes)

Choose one person to start your group time with prayer. In your own words, thank God for designing all of us with purpose and dignity. Ask God to make his presence evident in your time together and to use the Scriptures to unearth any theological weeds buried in our souls.

Scripture Reading (2 minutes)

Have one person read the following passage aloud:

JOHN 20:1–18 NLT

Early on Sunday morning, while it was still dark, Mary Magdalene came to the tomb and found that the stone had been rolled away from the entrance. She ran and found Simon Peter and the other disciple, the one whom Jesus loved. She said, "They have taken the Lord's body out of the tomb, and we don't know where they have put him!"

Peter and the other disciple started out for the tomb. They were both running, but the other disciple outran Peter and reached the tomb first. He stooped and looked in and saw the linen wrappings lying there, but he didn't go in. Then Simon Peter arrived and went inside. He also noticed the linen wrappings lying there, while the cloth that had covered Jesus' head was folded up and lying apart from the other wrappings. Then the disciple who had reached the tomb first also went in, and he saw and believed—for until then they still hadn't understood the Scriptures that said Jesus must rise from the dead. Then they went home.

Mary was standing outside the tomb crying, and as she wept, she stooped and looked in. She saw two white-robed angels, one sitting at the head and the other at the foot of the place where the body of Jesus had been lying. "Dear woman, why are you crying?" the angels asked her.

"Because they have taken away my Lord," she replied, "and I don't know where they have put him."

She turned to leave and saw someone standing there. It was Jesus, but she didn't recognize him. "Dear woman, why are you crying?" Jesus asked her. "Who are you looking for?"

She thought he was the gardener. "Sir," she said, "if you have taken him away, tell me where you have put him, and I will go and get him."

"Mary!" Jesus said.

She turned to him and cried out, "Rabboni!" (which is Hebrew for "Teacher").

"Don't cling to me," Jesus said, "for I haven't yet ascended to the Father. But go find my brothers and tell them, 'I am ascending to my Father and your Father, to my God and your God.'"

Mary Magdalene found the disciples and told them, "I have seen the Lord!" Then she gave them his message.

Watch Session 2 Video (15 minutes)

Video Notes

The first three words of John's Gospel say: "In the beginning."

Genesis starts the same way: "In the beginning."

John uses his Gospel as a parallel work to the first book of the Bible, Genesis.

Some scholars would say John's Gospel is like a second Genesis or a second beginning.

In John's Gospel Mary Magdalene is highlighted as a model disciple in the resurrection story.

Group Activity (20 minutes)

The table that follows lists several observations of contrast between Eve and Mary Magdalene. As a group, fill in the blanks together. You can check page 119 for complete answers.

Eve (Genesis 2–3)	Mary Magdalene (John 20:1–18)
Eve is in the Garden of _____	Mary is in the garden _____
Eve is placed inside the Garden by _____	Mary comes to the garden by her own initiative
Eve was forbidden to eat the fruit during the day	Mary comes to the tomb when it is still _____ outside
Eve was created after Adam	Mary is the _____ person to see Jesus risen from the dead–before Peter, before John
Eve faced the fruit-producing tree of _____	Mary faced a tomb of _____
Eve initiated a curse of _____ for all people with her rebellion	Mary initiated the resurrection _____ for all people with her obedience
_____ approached Eve with cunning questions that sowed doubt	Angels greeted Mary and then Jesus himself appeared to her, and they asked compassion-ate questions that sowed hope
Eve hid her _____ shame from God's presence before she was ousted from Eden	Mary wept without shame in Jesus' presence, and it was Jesus' cloths that were missing
Eve was _____	Mary was commissioned
Eve rebelled	Mary obeyed

Group Discussion (20 minutes)

1. What have you been taught about Eve as it relates to all women?

2. What about Mary's story stands out most to you?

3. In the video, Kat referenced filming archeologists uncovering ancient ruins of Mary Magdalene's hometown. Metaphorically speaking, what gifts are you uncovering about yourself?

4. If Mary is the first preacher to literally bring the gospel message, how should that influence our communities of faith?

5. How would you describe your faith-life right now? (Sitting, Standing, Walking, Running, Limping)

6. In what area of your life do you need one of God's epic redos?

End in Prayer (2 minutes)

Every week moving forward, your group will use the super handy prayer cards in the back of this study guide. Write your name and a prayer request on one of the cards so that you can pass it to one of the other members of your group. I like to keep the card passed to me in my Bible or posted to my fridge to remind me to pray for that person. Choose one person to close your time together in prayer and thank God for his power to redeem any area of our lives.

Preview

Leader read next week's preview to group:

We developed your personal study time so that you will address these common messages holding women back from fulfilling Jesus' Great Commandment: (1) Marriage is a woman's greatest joy and motherhood her highest calling; (2) I am too much to handle; (3) I don't have a lot to offer God.

Suggested Reading in
No More Holding Back:

Chapter 2

STAY IN YOUR PLACE
PERSONAL STUDY

Part One

My Greatest Joy Is Marriage &
My Highest Calling Is Motherhood

On my journey to better understand Jesus' Great Commandment, I realized I was making a dangerous swap by replacing marriage and motherhood for the words in that short but powerful verse in Mark 12:30 which says to love the Lord with all our hearts, souls, minds, and strength. I paraphrased it to "love the Lord as Aaron's wife and Caleb's mommy."

Being Aaron's wife and Caleb's mom makes me happy, adds significance to my life, and I fill a purpose in those roles. However valuable and noble I find them, neither are worthy of golden calf status. Whether intended or not, sometimes the church communicates to women that marriage is our greatest joy and motherhood our highest calling. And sometimes, women like me believe it. Dethroning the idols of Christian marriage and motherhood does not in any way devalue the institution of marriage or family. It elevates God to his unrivaled throne.

If we look closely again at Jesus' first and second Great Commandments, we find that in Christ's priorities there is nothing that speaks to a particular role of wife or mother, husband or father, boss or subordinate, young or old. It simply says to love God with our all and share that love with others. If Jesus elevates this commandment above all the others, we should too. Plus, the Bible is full of examples of those who are unmarried and women and men without children who are seen, accepted, and purposed by God to work for the common good of all people.

One such influential single lady was Mary Magdalene, whom we looked at in session 1. She held the distinction of being the first person to share the good news of Jesus' resurrection. There is no mention of her husband or children in the narrative. Mary was used by God to herald the gospel, preach to the disciples, and to testify to the resurrection of Christ. You might even say she was the apostle to the apostles.

In the Old Testament, Miriam, Moses' sister, was not married and had no children, yet she played a key role in our faith history. Read Exodus chapter 15 and 1 Corinthians chapter 12.

➤ What does Exodus 15:19–21 describe?

➤ What title is given to Miriam in Exodus 15:20?

➤ According to 1 Corinthians 12:28, how does the gift of prophecy rank among the most influential and desirable of the spiritual gifts?

Miriam led the women of Israel in song and dance after crossing the Red Sea to celebrate and worship God for delivering them from the Egyptians. Many years after she rescued her baby brother, Moses, from the Nile River, God used Miriam's singing voice to lead the congregation in corporate worship. She was a prophet and leader in the nation of Israel.

Jesus said to "go, therefore, and make disciples of all nations, baptizing them in the name of the Father and of the Son and of the Holy Spirit" (Matthew 28:19 csb)." But I wonder if some of us process those words this way, "Go therefore and make disciples before you get married, and baptize in the name of the Father, Son, and Holy Spirit before you start a family." Jesus said he came to give life and give it in abundance (John 10:10), but I think many women feel as though Jesus came to give us married life and kids in abundance. The apostle Paul encouraged Christians to not grow weary in doing good (Galatians 6:9), and I think I many of my sisters in Christ have paraphrased that based on personal desire and the messages prevalent in churches so that it reads, "Do not grow weary; soon you will have a spouse and soon you will have a family." When Paul taught Christians that we were created in Christ Jesus for good works (Ephesians 2:10), do we reshape that timeless truth to mean women were created just for a marriage and a family?

Internalizing the Scriptures is partly about the verses we hear in church and the way our leaders interpret and apply them in their teaching, but it's also partly how we process those truths through our lived experience. The idolization of marriage and motherhood is a result of both. In direct opposition to the idolatrous idea that godly women find satisfaction only in matrimony, Jesus is the unmarried embodiment of joy.

In my perfect world, I imagine a church that simultaneously and confidently affirms parents, spouses, *and* singles as indispensable to the mission of God. A place where all women's contributions to the body of Christ are valued, regardless of their age, stage, title, or relationship status. A place where missional mothers and devoted wives are not the only women on Jesus' A-Team. After all, Jesus excelled at making disciples without biological or adoptive children of his own and so did the apostle Paul.

There is no limit to what God can do in and through single women, women struggling with infertility, or women who choose never to have a family.

> How would our communities of faith change if we embraced all ages, stages, and roles as assignments from God?

➤ What role, age, and relationship status have you been idolizing? Take a moment and express to God you want that to change.

➤ Use the space below to process what God is asking you to do with these truths.

Part Two
I Am Too Much to Handle

"Be careful. The more a woman learns about the Scriptures, the less attractive she becomes to godly suitors because godly men want to lead their wives spiritually."

A young single woman approached me after a speaking engagement to confide that she had been accepted into a seminary and trusted her small group with this same news, when two college-aged men from her group explained that she should be "careful" about this decision. They applauded her desire to know God more, study the Scriptures, and fulfill her calling, but . . . "the stronger a wife is, the harder it is to be her spiritual leader." Not only is this statement untrue, it contradicts everything in the Great Commandment, Jesus' summary of godly living.

She was expressing something I hear often: she said that if a godly woman truly invests her all into her relationship with Christ, she lessens her chances of finding or keeping a godly husband. She tearfully explained she felt like she was "too much to handle." Sometimes the too-much-to-handle-struggle is about us trying to reconcile gifts of leadership, strong passion for God, or marketplace success with Christian culture or traditional gender roles. Sometimes it's because we think strong female Christians will be unable to submit to authority.

Although we probably *know* that godliness is always a good thing for all people at all times, I wonder if we truly *believe* it. *Strong* leaders do not struggle to submit; *bad* leaders do. Submission is not hard for *strong* women (or men); it's hard for *prideful* women (and men). Let's take a look at several "too much to handle" women in the Bible whom God held in high regard.

Deborah

Serving in judgeship of the nation of Israel, Deborah was a woman of valor leading the people of God with wisdom and courage. Read Judges 3–4.

> List four things you learn about Deborah from Judges 4:4–5

1. _____

2. _____

(cont.)

3. _____

4. _____

She wasn't just the lone woman to judge Israel; she also held the unique dual function of both fiery judge and authoritative prophet.[1] Similar to the reign of kings, she ruled over the military as judge, and she spoke with authority on behalf of God to his people as a prophetess. And she wasn't God's plan B. That much is clear from the text. God considered her an indispensable asset. He chose her to lead.

I'm bringing up Deborah's story to point out the fact that she was a strong woman *and* married. And we don't see any indication from the Scriptures that her success as a leader was against God's plan or getting in the way of a healthy marriage. Deborah wasn't too much to handle in God's eyes, even though she had national influence, even though her people recognized her leadership, and she delivered the Word of God to his people with authority. Let's make room in our churches and workplaces for women like Deborah. Because God did.

New Testament Disciples

Consider the band of women traveling with Jesus. Read Luke chapter 8.

➤ According to Luke 8:1–3, who traveled with Jesus in addition to the twelve male disciples?

➤ How did they support Jesus?

These women disciples not only followed Jesus, absorbing his teachings, they actually offered their funds to support his mission. Examples such as these show us that a woman's passion for her work, success on the job, or willingness to follow Jesus is not a negative.

Maybe we've overemphasized a woman's submissive role and in doing so lost sight of the fact that submission is *not* the hallmark of a Christian woman's character. The fruit of the Spirit is the hallmark of a Christian, male or female (pause here to look up and read Galatians 5).

Instead of asking if this woman can be led, we should ask, "Is this woman *Spirit*-led?" Instead of asking if she can submit, we should ask, "To *whom* does she submit?" And the answer should be, the Spirit. Women can and should be mighty and humble simultaneously because Jesus was.

For every woman out there thinking she is too much to handle, maybe she should think this way instead: How can I use what God has given to me to bring him glory and to work for the common good of all people?

We can't play small. And not because we are a big deal—quite the opposite. We can't play small because God's mission to reconcile all people to himself is too important.

2 CORINTHIANS 5:18–20 NLT

And all of this is a gift from God, who brought us back to himself through Christ. And God has given us this task of reconciling people to him. For God was in Christ, reconciling the world to himself, no longer counting people's sins against them. And he gave us this wonderful message of reconciliation. So we are Christ's ambassadors; God is making his appeal through us. We speak for Christ when we plead, "Come back to God!"

You were handcrafted with every single part of your personality, disposition, and wiring for the good works God intended for you to carry out.

EPHESIANS 2:10 NIV

For we are God's handiwork, created in Christ Jesus to do good works, which God prepared in advance for us to do.

➤ How can you use what God has given to you to bring him glory and to work for the common good of all people?

➤ Make a list for yourself of all the ways this week's Scripture has encouraged you to boldly embrace who you really are in Christ. Photocopy the page and keep it close. Reference the list every time you question, doubt, or feel insecure—in other words, OFTEN.

Because Jesus Says I Am Good "As Is"....

List as many positive things you can think of about yourself because Jesus already thinks them.

Part Three
I Don't Have a Lot to Offer

Maybe you are in a life season of abundant blessings, comfort, joy, and prosperity. Glory to God! He is the giver of all good gifts (James 1:17). Savor these treasures. Anticipate more days like this in your future. Or maybe you are grieved, anxious, confused, your body is failing you, and you want to give up. Theoretically, many of us know that we don't need to clean up before we meet with God, enjoy his presence, or experience his favor. But in practice, I like to wait until I'm in a "good place" to give back, serve my community, or take a risk.

No sooner do we set the bar higher for our great priorities of loving God and loving others than we second-guess our ability to fulfill them. Out of fear that we bring too little to the table, we reveal through our lack of confidence that our value system is much different from God's. He values the small, treasures the insignificant, and elevates the humble. In our world of all or nothing, Jesus teaches us "all" does not equate to "a lot."

After a scribe approached Jesus in the temple courts to ask which command is the most important of all, Jesus moved the conversation from the temple courts into the court for women,[2] where the priests had set up offering receptacles. The same audience listening to the greatest commandments were now following Christ into a different part of the temple so that he could give a teaching illustration. Read Mark 12:28–44.

➤ According to Mark 12:41–44, what is Jesus watching after he teaches about the Great Commandment?

➤ Who does Jesus instruct his disciples to learn from?

➤ Why does Jesus count the poor widow's contribution "more" than the donations of the rich crowds?

Watching many people contribute, Jesus called his listeners' attention to a poor widow giving out of her poverty as if to illustrate exactly what type of contribution he is looking for from all of us. As the least valuable person in her world, the widow donated her mite in a mighty act of surrender. Her culture overlooked her as the lowest class of society, the most vulnerable gender, insignificant to anyone of importance, and lacking the financial means to make a difference. But Jesus zoomed in on her gift as an example of true discipleship.

Noted theologian J. R. Edwards added valuable commentary to the scene:

> In purely financial terms, the value of her offering is negligible—and unworthy of compare to the sums of the wealthy donors. But in the divine exchange rate things look differently. That which made no difference in the books of the temple is immortalized in the Book of Life. How powerfully ironic is the word "more" in Mark's description. Everything about this woman has been described in terms of less, particularly in comparison to the scribes and wealthy crowd. And yet, the contrast between her genuine piety and faith and the pretense of the wealthy is beyond compare.[3]

Giving of ourselves when we have little to offer, when it's all we've got, is worthy of God's commendation—even when it seems our economy deems it the least valuable gift. Every gift counts, especially those that come from hard-up places.

➤ Circle which of these you are struggling with now.

- Broken heart
- Troubled soul
- Confused mind
- Weakened strength

To all the women nursing broken hearts, serving on empty does not equate with failure. Our Savior experienced heartache too. He knows our pain. He sees our suffering. And he joins us there. "He heals the brokenhearted and binds up their wounds" (Psalm 147:3 NIV). To all you wavering women still choosing to flip the pages of this book, keep at it. Maybe instead of having it all together, we bring our disillusioned self to Jesus with confidence in his heaven-oriented value system. To all the women perplexed about a passage of Scripture, annoyed by one of the stories of the Bible, flustered by the injustice we see in the Scriptures, or disenchanted by our spiritual leaders—you are human, and real life doesn't always make sense immediately. To all the women conserving their energy for a time in the future when they can really make a difference, remember what Paul says in 2 Corinthians 12:10, "when I am weak, then I am strong" (NIV).

Serving God will at times mean loving him with a broken heart, troubled soul, confused mind, and weakened strength. And that is okay, more than okay. Such sacrificial service has eternal significance.

Pitted against our intentions to follow God we face a very real Enemy telling us we are not enough, we don't have enough, and this is not the right time. He whispers we need to clean up, shape up, gear up, and get more of something before we can serve Jesus. He sticks his nose up to our failings and recommends sitting this season out because of the legitimate constraints in our schedules, bank accounts, or emotional capacity.

But Jesus runs his kingdom with the currency of love. Our world obsesses with surplus while Jesus cheers for those of us giving from our emotional and financial poverty. We may not have a lot to offer, but we can give him everything we've got.

Because, with him, you have more than enough.

> What would it look like to offer the little you have to God?

➤ In what ways would your daily life change or be altered? Would anyone be able to see a difference? Would it matter? Why or why not?

➤ List three or four actionable steps you can take this week toward offering God the little you have.

PART TWO

THE CALL TO
LOVE GOD

THREE

ALL YOUR HEART

Group Time

Leader read Kat's message to the group:

As I considered how we could live up to Jesus' call in Mark 12:30 to love God with all our hearts, I went to the Word of God for direction. Before looking up most of the times the word *heart* was used in the Bible, I was expecting confirmation that ladies need to control their feelings, because I've grown up hearing how much more emotional women are than men and how much more relational we are than our brothers in Christ. While keeping my feelings in check and directing my affection toward Christ is a worthy goal, it's not the extent of loving God with all my heart.

I was surprised that even though the word *heart* appears more than a thousand times in the Bible, it rarely describes just our feelings or one of our internal organs. Instead, many of the authors of Scripture use the term more broadly to mean "our truest inner selves." Think about that. Our truest inner selves can sometimes be buried beneath our insecurities, our talents, the opinions of others, or even contrast what we say we believe. When authors of Scripture used the word *heart*, they intended for us to envision the raw, honest truth about our whole lives.

Start with Prayer (2 minutes)

Choose one person to open in prayer. Ask God to teach each of you more about loving him with all of your hearts.

Scripture Reading (2 minutes)

Select volunteers to read the following passages:

ROMANS 5:1–5 CSB

Therefore, since we have been declared righteous by faith, we have peace with God through our Lord Jesus Christ. We have also obtained access through Him by faith into this grace in which we stand, and we rejoice in the hope of the glory of God. And not only that, but we also rejoice in our afflictions, because we know that affliction produces endurance, endurance produces proven character, and proven character produces hope. This hope will not disappoint us, because God's love has been poured out in our hearts through the Holy Spirit who was given to us.

2 CORINTHIANS 4:16–18 CSB

Therefore we do not give up. Even though our outer person is being destroyed, our inner person is being renewed day by day. For our momentary light affliction is producing for us an absolutely incomparable eternal weight of glory. So we do not focus on what is seen, but on what is unseen. For what is seen is temporary, but what is unseen is eternal.

LUKE 18:1–8 ESV

And he told them a parable to the effect that they ought always to pray and not lose heart. He said, "In a certain city there was a judge who neither feared God nor respected man. And there was a widow in that city who kept coming to him and saying, 'Give me justice against my adversary.' For a while he refused, but afterward he said to himself, 'Though I neither fear God nor respect man, yet because this widow keeps bothering me, I will give her justice, so that she will not beat me down by her continual coming.'" And the Lord said, "Hear what the unrighteous judge says. And will not God give justice to his elect, who cry to him day and night? Will he delay long over them? I tell you, he will give justice to them speedily. Nevertheless, when the Son of Man comes, will he find faith on earth?"

Watch Session 2 Video (15 minutes)

Video Notes

Building cardio strength is a physical discipline for our bodies but can also teach a sacred spiritual lesson about loving God with all our hearts.

Loving God with all our hearts is so much more than Jesus-focused mushy gushy stuff.

It's about loving God with our truest inner selves.

The word *heart* comes up several times when the authors of the Bible talk about how hard it is to not give up.

Some Bibles translate the phrase *lose heart* as "do not give up or don't grow weary, become discouraged, be spiritless, despairing, exhausted, or faint."

Group Discussion (35 minutes)

Choose a volunteer to reread:

ROMANS 5:1–5 CSB

Therefore, since we have been declared righteous by faith, we have peace with God through our Lord Jesus Christ. We have also obtained access through him by faith into this grace in which we stand, and we rejoice in the hope of the glory of God. And not only that, but we also rejoice in our afflictions, because we know that affliction produces endurance, endurance produces proven character, and proven character produces hope. This hope will not disappoint us, because God's love has been poured out in our hearts through the Holy Spirit who was given to us.

➤ What hardship in your life eventually led to rejoicing and why?

➤ Why do perseverance and proven character produce Christ-centered hope in our lives?

➤ What has been the most hope-filled season of your life and why?

Choose a volunteer to reread:

2 CORINTHIANS 4:16–18 CSB

Therefore we do not give up. Even though our outer person is being destroyed, our inner person is being renewed day by day. For our momentary light affliction is producing for us an absolutely incomparable eternal weight of glory. So we do not focus on what is seen, but on what is unseen. For what is seen is temporary, but what is unseen is eternal.

➤ According to 2 Corinthians 4:16–18, enduring challenges in life means focusing our attention on our eternal hope. What helps you keep your focus on your eternal hope?

➤ If you feel like you have lost heart, share that with your group so that your group leader can pause and pray over you right now.

Choose a volunteer to reread:

LUKE 18:1–8 ESV

And he told them a parable to the effect that they ought always to pray and not lose heart. He said, "In a certain city there was a judge who neither feared God nor respected man. And there was a widow in that city who kept coming to him and saying, 'Give me justice against my adversary.' For a while he refused, but afterward he said to himself, 'Though I neither fear God nor respect man, yet because this widow keeps bothering me, I will give her justice, so that she will not beat me down by her continual coming.'" And the Lord said, "Hear what the unrighteous judge says. And will not God give justice to his elect, who cry to him day and night? Will he delay long over them? I tell you, he will give justice to them speedily. Nevertheless, when the Son of Man comes, will he find faith on earth?"

➤ For the second time in our study we are looking at one of Jesus' parables where a widow is the example of godliness. Why do you think Jesus uses a widow to talk about not losing heart?

➤ What does Jesus prescribe as the way to avoid burnout and discouragement?

➤ Brainstorm all the differences between God and the unrighteous judge.

End in Prayer (5 minutes)

Every week your group will use the prayer cards in the back of this study guide. Write your name on one of the cards and a prayer request that you can pass to one of the other members of your group. I like to keep the card passed to me in my Bible or posted to my fridge to remind me to pray for that person.

Choose one person to close your time together in prayer and ask God for more of his sustaining power as we all face circumstances tempting us to lose heart.

Suggested Reading in
No More Holding Back:

Chapter 6

Session Three

ALL YOUR HEART
PERSONAL STUDY

Part One
God's Clean Slate

As the proud owner of many full notebooks, I get a real kick when cracking open a brand new one. The best part is turning to that first empty page to date the inaugural entry. Free from the wear and tear of life, page one is clean and brimming with potential. What new things will God teach today? What ancient story will be relevant to my life today? What message is he trying to communicate? It seems to me God probably has a similar excitement when he finds us willing to listen to him. God is capable of writing a good story through our lives, and the inscriptions of his grace start with the clean slate of a new heart.

In the ancient Near Eastern culture, which is the backdrop for the Scriptures, people believed their hearts needed replacing. They were right. If our actions originate there, we need a fresh start. If we are going to live with integrity and purpose, we need a holy surgery to remove our sinful tendencies, one accomplished through Christ's death on the cross. Our Great Surgeon used his own blood on the cross to complete the supernatural transplant we all need.

We see this theme in the wisdom literature of Proverbs.

➤ Read Proverbs 3:1–6. According to these verses, what do godly parents instruct their children to do with loyalty and faithfulness?

➤ Turn to Proverbs 7:3 in your Bible and read it. According to this verse, where does the teacher say to tie good teachings?

When we read the word *tablet*, we might think of a device we use to do Instagram stalking late at night before bed. But tablets would have propelled a Jewish reader back to the Exodus story where God wrote the Ten Commandments on tablets of stone in Exodus 20 and 34. Look up and read Ezekiel 11:19–20.

➤ What did the prophet Ezekiel say the stone tablets would eventually turn into (v. 19)?

➤ What did the prophet Jeremiah have to say about the same topic in Jeremiah 31:33?

We can't do the right thing, have the correct motives, or fulfill the Great Commandment without a new heart. Praise God that happens when we become Christians. Remember what Romans 5:5 says, "God's love has been poured out in our hearts through the Holy Spirit who was given to us" (NIV). Plus, he's got the right tools for the most hardened people. "For the word of God is living and active, sharper than any two-edged sword, piercing to the division of soul and of spirit, of joints and of marrow, and discerning the thoughts and intentions of the heart" (Hebrews 4:12 ESV). God can get through to us, even those who feel like one more touch will shatter them. His tender care makes the swap. We can trust him.

➤ If your heart were a brand new journal and this were your inaugural entry, what would it describe about the state of your heart?

Part Two
More Than Mushy-Gushy Stuff

I sifted through commentaries and lexicons to find that the meaning of *heart* in the Bible includes our whole personality and disposition with an emphasis on reason and will. The best way I could summarize my findings on the word is that our heart is the driving force behind our actions.[1] Loving God with all our hearts is not just feeling love toward God or redirecting misguided feelings back to God. It's about letting our love for him determine how we live.

➤ Look up Mark 2:8 and write down Jesus' question to the scribes:

Isn't it interesting that he asked about *thinking* rather than *feeling*? I usually separate those two into different categories, because lots of personality tests make thinking and feeling a binary choice. The truth is, thinking and feeling are deeply intertwined. Jesus' point is that our thought life and emotional well-being are interconnected. Read Mark 7:14–23.

➤ What does Jesus say comes out of people's hearts in Mark 7:21–23?

What a list! Jesus is saying our behavior reveals the contents of our hearts. Now, turn to Luke 6:37–45.

➤ How will we know what is in someone's heart according Jesus in Luke 6:45?

Verse after verse points to the fact that our behavior reveals our authentic selves, which is the meaning of *heart* in the Bible. Loving God with all our hearts is so much more than Jesus-focused mushy-gushy stuff. It's about loving God with our truest inner selves and letting that love shine through our lives and determine our actions.

➤ Using only examples from last week, what does your behavior reveal about your heart?

➤ Using only examples from last week, what does your speech reveal about your heart?

➤ Use this time and space to confess to God how you would like him to change your heart and how willing you are to participate in the process.

Part Three
Purify Your Heart

One of Jesus' followers was a brave and fiery preacher named Stephen. His unique title, the first Christian martyr, should draw our attention to his last sermon. As he faced his death, he continued to declare to people, a lot like you and me, that they had "uncircumcised hearts."

ACTS 7:51 NIV

You stiff-necked people! Your hearts and ears are still uncircumcised. You are just like your ancestors: You always resist the Holy Spirit!

> Other than "uncircumcised hearts," how did Stephen describe the crowd listening to his sermon in Acts?

ROMANS 5:1–5 NIV

Therefore, since we have been justified through faith, we have peace with God through our Lord Jesus Christ, through whom we have gained access by faith into this grace in which we now stand. And we boast in the hope of the glory of God. Not only so, but we also glory in our sufferings, because we know that suffering produces perseverance; perseverance, character; and character, hope. And hope does not put us to shame, because God's love has been poured out into our hearts through the Holy Spirit, who has been given to us.

➤ According to these verses in Romans, into what has God's love been poured?

➤ How did it get there?

Thousands of years later we can read Stephen's choice words to discover the surest way to diagnose the condition of our hearts: to evaluate if we are resisting the Holy Spirit.

ACTS 7:54 NIV

When the members of the Sanhedrin heard this, they were furious and gnashed their teeth at him.

➤ According to this verse, how did the audience respond to Stephen's accusations?

Resisting the Holy Spirit can lead to rage in our hearts. You and I know rage. Maybe only for a brief moment or maybe a long, challenging season. We know what it's like to have anger and bitterness compounding daily circumstances that seem to justify our temperament.

JAMES 4:8 NIV

Come near to God and he will come near to you. Wash your hands, you sinners, and purify your hearts, you double-minded.

➤ According to James, what will be required of us to remove rage from our hearts?

I don't know how to purify my own heart, and neither did the author of Psalm 51. Notice his prayer in verse 10:

PSALM 51:10 CSB

God, create a clean heart for me and renew a steadfast spirit within me.

It's God who can create a clean heart for us. It's God who can renew in us a steadfast spirit. If you feel as though your heart is dirty, muddy, clouded, darkened, or hard, take heart. If we ask God, he is able to design a pure heart for us. A place where he can make his home with us.

FOUR

ALL YOUR SOUL

Group Time

Leader read Kat's message to the group:

We know that all living human beings have a soul, and some Bible experts would say we don't just *have* a soul, we *are* a living soul.[1] They are one in the same. Many times in the Old Testament, scholars actually translate the word *soul* as "life" because the two are inseparable.

The Holman Treasury of Key Bible Words says, "if we properly understand the profound meaning encapsulated in the word 'soul,' then the greatest of all commandments carries a far deeper significance than a surface reading would allow . . . We should love the Lord with the very fiber of our being, with everything that makes us human!"[2] If Jesus guides us to love him with all our souls, then he's looking for women to love him through all aspects of our lives—the good, the bad, and the ugly.

Start with Prayer (2 minutes)

Choose one person to start your group time in prayer. In your own words, thank God for loving us well through every season of life. And ask him to teach your group more about what it means to love God with all your souls.

Scripture Reading (3 minutes)

Select volunteers to read the following passages:

LUKE 1:26–38 CSB

In the sixth month, the angel Gabriel was sent by God to a town in Galilee called Nazareth, to a virgin engaged to a man named Joseph, of the house of David. The virgin's name was Mary. And the angel came to her and said, "Greetings, favored woman! The Lord is with you." But she was deeply troubled by this statement, wondering what kind of greeting this could be. Then the angel told her: "Do not be afraid, Mary, for you have found favor with God. Now listen: You will conceive and give birth to a son, and you will call his name Jesus. He will be great and will be called the Son of the Most High, and the Lord God will give him the throne of his father David. He will reign over the house of Jacob forever, and his kingdom will have no end." Mary asked the angel, "How can this be, since I have not had sexual relations with a man?" The angel replied to her:

"The Holy Spirit will come upon you, and the power of the Most High will overshadow you. Therefore, the holy One to be born will be called the Son of God. And consider your relative Elizabeth—even she has conceived a son in her old age, and this is the sixth month for her who was called childless. For nothing will be impossible with God." "I am the Lord's servant," said Mary. "May it be done to me according to your word." Then the angel left her.

LUKE 1:46–55 CSB

And Mary said: My soul proclaims the greatness of the Lord, and my spirit has rejoiced in God my Savior, because he has looked with favor on the humble condition of his slave. Surely, from now on all generations will call me blessed, because the Mighty One has done great things for me, and his name is holy. His mercy is from generation to generation on those who fear him. He has done a mighty deed with his arm; he has scattered the proud because of the thoughts of their hearts; he has toppled the mighty from their thrones and exalted the lowly. He has satisfied the hungry with good things and sent the rich away empty. He has helped his servant Israel, mindful of his mercy, just as he spoke to our ancestors, to Abraham and his descendants forever.

LAMENTATIONS 3:17–20 NIV

I have been deprived of peace;
>   I have forgotten what prosperity is.
So I say, "My splendor is gone
>   and all that I had hoped from the LORD."
I remember my affliction and my wandering,
>   the bitterness and the gall.
I well remember them,
>   and my soul is downcast within me.

Watch Session 4 Video (15 minutes)

Video Notes

Mary was ready to believe God in season and out.

Her circumstances didn't dictate her level of faith.

Jesus is looking for women to love him through all aspects of life—the good, the bad, and the ugly.

Lamentations is a book of the Bible devoted to hopeful sorrow.

Crying out to our Savior with hurt and anger is not only permissible, it's an act of worship.

Group Discussion (35 minutes)

1. Describe a time when you experienced an uncertain future or a scary present. How did God help you through it?

2. Knowing that many Bible translators use the words *life* and *soul* interchangeably, how does that influence how you think about God's Great Commandment to love him with all your soul?

3. How could the church cultivate attitudes of compassion for people who have troubled souls?

4. Why do you think Mary's soul was able to proclaim the greatness of the Lord just moments after receiving frightening and life-altering news?

5. What are some of God's promises to us that should comfort our souls?

6. How can we celebrate God's faithfulness when life doesn't turn out the way we expected?

7. What does it look like when you lament?

End in Prayer (5 minutes)

Use the prayer cards in the back of this study guide and choose one person to close your time together in prayer, asking God to comfort anyone with a troubled soul.

Suggested Reading in
No More Holding Back:

Chapter 7

ALL YOUR SOUL
PERSONAL STUDY

Part One
Celebrating Jubilee

The word *soul* is used more than two hundred times in the Bible. In my research, I printed out every verse with that word and placed them side by side for comparison. Immediately, I noticed that the passages from the Old and New Testaments sound a lot alike. Beyond all of them containing the word *soul*, many of the similarities traced back to the concept of "Jubilee" introduced in Leviticus.

What is Jubilee? It's a season on the Jewish calendar that serves as a reminder that things are not as they should be, that we need a Savior to clean up our messes right now, and that God eventually is going to make all things new. It teaches us to be hopeful in times of trouble, to be expectant when the odds are against us, and to worship God when life doesn't make sense. Jubilee celebrates God in every season of life.

We can glean a lot from studying a number of heroes of the faith in Scripture who knew the importance of Jubilee and show us exactly what it means to love God with our whole soul.

Moses

In a pivotal scene, found in Leviticus 25, Moses gave the details of his meeting with the one true God, Yahweh, who had instructed Moses to celebrate the Year of Jubilee.

➤ What did God say to Moses about the seventh year in Leviticus 25:1–5?

The Lord went on to teach Moses about sacred seasons. Every seven years, the land and people would enjoy rest for a whole year and the pattern would repeat seven times. Then in the fiftieth year, they were to rest in another yearlong Sabbath called Jubilee.

Jubilee was supposed to include freeing slaves, forgiving debtors, feeding the hungry, supporting the poor, and bringing joy to the brokenhearted. Jubilee shows God's love for his children and points to a future freedom he has for them.

David

King David, who recently repented of murder and adultery, could still worship God with all that was in him, because he knew God's redemptive power to save our lives.

➤ Write out King David's song lyric from Psalm 103:1–2.

➤ According to Psalm 103:6, who will enjoy the Lord's righteousness and justice?

This ancient song of deliverance certainly would have reached the prophet Isaiah's ears before he prophesied about Jubilee.

Isaiah

Speaking of the future Messiah, Isaiah's prophecy teaches more about Jubilee.

➤ List everything the future Messiah would do according to Isaiah 61:1–3.

Jubilee was supposed to be for a season. A Jewish reader would have had her hair blown back to hear that Isaiah's message of freedom for the poor, the oppressed, the enslaved, the brokenhearted, the despairing, and the mourning could come to fruition in a non-Jubilee year.

What we've learned together today is that Jubilee was supposed to set prisoners free, release captives from bondage, forgive debtors their debt, and to elevate the poor. Moses teaches about Jubilee (Leviticus 25); David sings about it (Psalm 103); and then Isaiah prophesies about it in Isaiah 61. What we will see in Part 2 is a connection to Jesus and his mother, Mary.

Part Two
Mary the Mother of God

If any woman in the Scriptures exemplifies what it means to love God with all her soul, it's Mary, Jesus' mother. According to Dr. Timothy Ralston, she ranks as the fourth most described person in the New Testament behind Jesus, Paul, and Peter.[1] All four Gospel writers give us part of Mary's story to show us that she's a model disciple of Jesus, a humble servant of God, and fully committed to her faith.

One of the Gospel writers, Luke, does something unique with the birth announcement of Jesus. He brings us into the narrative in a way we can experience it from a woman's perspective and allows the story to be a woman-only scene, which are both really rare in the Bible. The only other times the people of God have heard a woman singing praises for salvation is through Miriam, Moses' sister, who led the people of God in worship after crossing the Red Sea and receiving deliverance from the Egyptians (Exodus 15:21); Deborah, God's appointed judge and prophet, who helped Barak defeat the enemy (Judges 5); and Hannah, mother of the prophet Samuel, the last judge to rule Israel (1 Samuel 2:1–10). Luke's Gospel should be a mile marker for those of us pursing God. It should remind us that God gives voice to women, and Mary is joining an exclusive group of women of the Old Testament used by God as his agents of salvation.

The book of Luke tells the story of a young Jewish girl named Mary who was engaged to marry a man named Joseph (Luke 1). The angel Gabriel was sent by God to Nazareth, where Mary was living at the time to announce to Mary that, although she was a virgin, the Holy Spirit would come upon her and she would conceive and give birth to the Messiah. He went on to explain that although she was deeply troubled by his statement she should not be afraid. Okay, angel. He explained this turn of events was a blessing from God. Mary's son was going to be the Son of God and his name would be Jesus.

▶ How does Mary respond in Luke 1:46–55?

Where did Mary find this kind of faith in the moment? Why did she respond the way she did? I think it's because her faith was solid. She knew Jubilee was coming one way or another. And she was ready to believe God in season and out. Her circumstances didn't dictate her level of faith. She believed the slaves would be set free, even if at the moment she was still a lowly servant herself. She had faith the hungry were going to be fed, even though she saw poverty all around her. She trusted that the brokenhearted would find joy again, even though her own life plan was going to be redirected. Mary knew the God who could accomplish all of this. When he showed up and revealed the next steps in his plan, she was filled with faith even though her soul must have been troubled. Notice that Mary's magnificat, her song of praise to God, includes familiar phrases that relate to Jubilee. **Circle the phrases below.**

LUKE 1:48, 50–53 CSB

He has looked with favor on the humble condition of his servant. . . . His mercy is from generation to generation on those who fear him. He has done a mighty deed with his arm; he has scattered the proud because of the thoughts of their hearts; he has toppled the mighty from their thrones and exalted the lowly. He has satisfied the hungry with good things and sent the rich away empty.

Jesus' mom's famous anthem reveals what an incredible theologian she was and how great an impact she had on her Son. He would grow up and make her song come alive. Mary sang about Jubilee because she knew Moses' teaching; she'd heard David's songs; and she was familiar with Isaiah's prophecies. But Jesus is it. Jesus *is* Jubilee.

> What part of Isaiah 61 did Jesus read in Luke 4:16–21?

(Drops microphone to stage.)

My brain can barely compute the significance of this moment, and I wish I had been present to see the faces of those within earshot who were getting their minds blown. Jubilee is here now. His name is Jesus.

➤ Write out the praise that is flooding your soul knowing that Jesus is Jubilee.

Part Three
Troubled Souls

Mary's story may be very different from yours, but I bet you know what it's like to have an uncertain future or a scary present. And I want to remind you that now's the time to stay connected to God. If your life is hard, in a way you can't describe to even your closest friends or family, guess what? Jesus will understand.

He wants us to trust him when we get a promotion at work, when we fail miserably on a project, and when we slog through an ordinary nine-to-five job. He calls us to enjoy him on an emotional mountaintop and in the pit of despair, and even when we feel blah. He wants stay-at-home moms to praise him when the baby takes their first steps, when they come home from school with a failing grade, and during the long trudge of sleepless nights and early morning wake-up calls.

God desires our companionship when we are easy to talk to, when we feel like giving him the silent treatment, or when we repeat the same old conversation we had with him yesterday. In fact, God longs for us to bring him all our highs, lows, and everything in between. To rejoice in God through it all is the kind of commitment God seeks. Loving God with all our soul is praising him through every season of life.

And, spoiler alert, that doesn't mean our praise will always feel glad. Sometimes it will be laments. The book of Lamentations is devoted to hopeful sorrow and bursting with pain—rip-your-heart-out, tear-your-clothes, lift-your-fist-to-God pain. Squirming through depressing prayers, I found myself shocked and encouraged by the author's authenticity.

➤ Using the author's phrases, describe what inner turmoil feels like according to Lamentations 3:17–20.

Crying out to our Savior with hurt and anger is not only permissible, it's an act of worship. As our tears fall and our heads hang low, our cries directed to the living God prove our faith; we believe he exists and that reaching out to him will ease our suffering. Faith *is* for the faint of heart. Hope *is* for the souls deprived of peace.

➤ What lament-filled phrase is repeated four times in Psalm 13:1–3?

Soulful living doesn't mean we spend our days humming happy tunes about the good in our lives, acting continuously downcast about the bad, or mourning the ugly. Soulful living encompasses all of that and everything in between. Aspiring to fulfill the Greatest Commandment means honoring God when life gets real, through thick and thin.

➤ How did Jesus lament to the Father in Mark 14:36?

➤ What are you lamenting right now?

FIVE

ALL YOUR MIND

Group Time

Leader read Kat's message to the group:

We've spent the last few weeks digging into Jesus' Great Commandment in Mark 12:30 where he tells a scribe the most important thing a Christian can do: Love God with all their heart, all their soul, all their mind, and all their strength.

This week we are going to look carefully at the word *mind* in the Bible. What we are going to see is that in addition to a new heart willing to do the right thing and a soul able to celebrate God when life gets real, God redeems our minds too—so that we can understand the truth of the gospel and so that we can keep our minds pure. God also redeems our minds so that we stay open to new ideas, constantly ready for God to *change* our minds through his Word.

If accepting the meaning of heart and soul was a challenge, becoming mindful Jesus-followers is going to be a battle. Second Corinthians 10:5 says, "We demolish arguments and every proud thing that is raised up against the knowledge of God, and we take every thought captive to obey Christ" (CSB). Sounds like thought-life fight club to me.

Jesus' call to focus our minds on Christ is more straightforward than the other portions of the Greatest Commandment we have studied so far, but much more convicting.

Start with Prayer (2 minutes)

Ask God to open your minds to understand his truths and where it's necessary to change us to become more like Christ.

Scripture Reading (3 minutes)

Select volunteers to read the following passages:

ROMANS 8:5–8 CSB

For those who live according to the flesh have their minds set on the flesh, but those who live according to the Spirit, have their minds set on the things of the Spirit. Now mind-set of the flesh is death, but the mind-set of the Spirit is life and peace. The mind-set of the flesh is hostile to God because it does not submit itself to God's law. Indeed it is unable to do so. Those who are in the flesh cannot please God.

EPHESIANS 4:21–24, 31–32 CSB

You heard about him and were taught by him, as the truth is in Jesus, to take off your former way of life, the old self that is corrupted by deceitful desires, to be renewed in the spirit of your minds, and to put on the new self, the one created according to God's likeness in righteousness and purity of the truth. . . . Let all bitterness, anger and wrath, shouting and slander must be removed from you, along with all malice. And be kind and compassionate to one another, forgiving one another, just as God also forgave you in Christ.

ROMANS 12:1–2 TPT

Beloved friends, what should be our proper response to God's marvelous mercies? I encourage you to surrender yourselves to God to be his sacred, living sacrifices. And live in holiness, experiencing all that delights his heart. For this becomes your genuine expression of worship.

Stop imitating the ideals and opinions of the culture around you, but be inwardly transformed by the Holy Spirit through a total reformation of how you think. This will empower you to discern God's will as you live a beautiful life, satisfying and perfect in his eyes.

COLOSSIANS 1:21–23 CSB

Once you were alienated and hostile in your minds expressed in your evil actions. But now he has reconciled you by his physical body through his death, to present you holy, faultless, and blameless before him—if indeed you remain grounded and steadfast in the faith and are not shifted away from the hope of the gospel that you heard.

Watch Session 5 Video (15 minutes)

Video Notes

We are given the mind of Christ when we come to faith in Jesus.

The mind of Christ enables us to understand the Scriptures and it helps us keep our mind from temptation.

Women who love God with all their mind are open to new ideas and allow God to transform their perspective.

For the Jewish people in the Old Testament, producing purity required a gruesome offering that cost the animals their lives.

Group Discussion (35 minutes)

Based on the Romans 8:5–8 Scripture reading:

➤ How does Paul describe the mind-set of the flesh? Give a concrete example of this from your life before knowing Christ as Savior.

➤ How does Paul describe the mind-set of the Spirit? Give a concrete example of this from your life before knowing Christ as Savior.

➤ How does Paul describe hostility toward God?

Based on the Ephesians 4:22–24, 31–32 Scripture reading:

➤ What is Paul's solution for Christians struggling with bitterness, anger, shouting, and slander?

➤ According to Paul, what kind of behavior reveals our minds are being renewed by the Spirit?

➤ If you feel like bitterness, anger, shouting, or slander are getting the better of you, pause to ask the group to lift up your struggle in prayer. God can help.

Based on the Romans 12:1–2 Scripture reading:

➤ What would it look like for you to surrender yourself to God to be his sacred, living sacrifice?

➤ What ideals and opinions of the culture around you are you imitating?

➤ If the Holy Spirit transformed the way you think about that cultural ideal/opinion, how would your life be different?

End in Prayer (5 minutes)

Use the prayer cards in the back of this study guide. Write your name on one of the cards and a prayer request that you can pass to one of the other members of your group. And then choose one person to close your time together in prayer, asking God to help you love him with all your mind. Ask him to empower you to discern his will and that you would be inwardly transformed by the Holy Spirit.

Suggested Reading in
No More Holding Back:

Chapter 8

ALL YOUR MIND
PERSONAL STUDY

Part One
Smart Female Disciples

I have heard people criticize women in the Gospels for their overly emotional responses to situations with Jesus. A closer look proves in each case that women normally assumed to be hysterical, impassioned, or sentimental actually think correctly about spiritual matters. Women have no advantage over men when applying their mind to Christ, but both genders have access to the Holy Spirit, which enlightens us to understand truth. But I will say, it seems the Gospel writers, under the inspiration of the Spirit, made a concerted effort to highlight female disciples making accurate judgment calls based on logical thought processes and astute comprehension of events. I think the Bible levels the playing field for women seeking to love God with all their minds.

For instance, in John 11 we read of Mary and Martha's brother, Lazarus, who fell deathly ill. Knowing that Jesus could fix the situation, the sisters pursued Jesus with the news. Strangely, he did not respond the way Mary and Martha would have hoped, delaying his arrival so long that Lazarus died. Four days after Lazarus's burial, Jesus arrived in the town of Bethany to find Mary and Martha distraught with grief, and understandably so. Their brother was dead.

> Read John chapter 11. According to verse 20, how did Martha and Mary respond to Jesus' arrival in Bethany?

Taking off to meet him, unable to wait one more minute to confront his indifference for their pain, Martha lamented, "Lord, if you had been here my brother wouldn't have died" (John 11:21 csb). Martha spoke the truth. We can't know for sure how she said those words or what her tone communicated about her emotions, but we read John's quotes to find that Martha knew what she was talking about.

Most of the sermons I've heard on this moment in our faith history revolve around Martha's sensitive response in her sorrow. We might even replay the events in our head to assume Martha was accusing Jesus with anger when she said, "If you had been here my brother wouldn't have died." But her comments are also another way of saying, "Your presence brings life," which is an admission of faith. If Jesus had been present when Lazarus fell ill, he could have healed him; that is true.

> What did Jesus tell Martha in verse 25?

Jesus proclaimed to Martha the life-altering news: he is the resurrection and the life and anyone who believes in him, even if they die, will live. And then he questioned Martha on this new information. "Do you believe this?" Martha confessed, "I believe you are the Messiah, the Son of God, who comes into the world" (v. 27 csb). Our hearts should quicken reading about the saving grace of Jesus making sense to someone. What a work of the Spirit.

Next, Jesus requested Mary's presence. Rushing to Jesus, Mary fell at her Savior's feet and told him the same thing Martha did. "Lord, if you had been here, my brother would not have died!" (v. 32). Comforting each other and hovering over their brother's dead body, the sisters had likely traded their sentiments during their lament.

> According to John 11:33, what was Mary doing while she threw herself at Jesus?

This may lead us to assume she spoke only through the lens of passion. But what if her tears and words were not only emotionally charged but also evidence that she understood the truth about the Messiah? If Peter had done that instead, would we interpret their comments differently?

> Read John 11:27 as well as Matthew 16:13–16. Write out the similarities between Martha's confession of faith and that of Peter's.

Mary and Martha are perfect examples of mindful women of God. Allowing the Holy Spirit to change their minds, they can receive and adopt a new point of view, and thus align with God himself on the matter and love him with all their hearts, souls, *and* minds.

> Besides this study guide, how are you seeking to love God with all your mind?

Part Two
Perceptive Christ-followers

Our death-conqueror, Jesus, raised Lazarus from the dead, proving he is the resurrection and the life. No doubt Mary, Martha, and Lazarus must have been overjoyed by Christ's miracle. It makes sense that the next time they saw Jesus in Bethany they threw a dinner party in his honor.

Read John 12:1–11.

➤ Based on verse 1, when did Jesus come to Bethany?

➤ What was Martha doing during the dinner party? (John 12:2)

➤ What was Lazarus doing during the dinner party? (John 12:2)

Think about sitting next to Lazarus at a dinner party. I wouldn't be able to stop staring. People, he was dead. Then Jesus made him alive. What else is there to talk about at a dinner party with both Lazarus and Jesus present?

At some point during the meal, Mary took a pound of expensive oil, worth one year's income, to anoint Jesus' feet and then wiped his feet with her hair.

➤ How did Judas respond to Mary's anointing? (John 12:4–5)

➤ What was Judas's motivation? (John 12:6)

➤ What did Jesus say to reprimand Judas? (John 12:7)

The disciples got angry about Mary's wasted treasure and the missed opportunity to help the poor with such a valuable commodity. But what they failed to recognize was that they are the poor, the spiritually poor. What the disciples judged a reckless act was just the opposite, according to Jesus. It was the most appropriate response to her Messiah.

We find the same story in the Gospel of Mark, chapter 14. Notice the way the New English Translation translates the story:

MARK 14:3–9 NET

Now while Jesus was in Bethany at the house of Simon the leper, reclining at the table, a woman came with an alabaster jar of costly aromatic oil from pure nard. After breaking open the jar, she poured it on his head. But some who were present indignantly said to one another, "Why this waste of expensive ointment? It could have been sold for more than three hundred silver coins and the money given to the poor!" So they spoke angrily to her. But Jesus said, "Leave her alone. Why are you bothering her? She has done a good service for me. For you will always have the poor with you, and you can do good for them whenever you want. But you will not always have me! She did what she could. She anointed my body beforehand for burial. I tell you the truth, wherever the gospel is proclaimed in the whole world, what she has done will also be told in memory of her."

➤ What two things did Jesus say Mary accomplished? (Mark 14:8)

➤ Where will Mary's story be told in memory of her? (Mark 14:9)

I noticed many contrasts between Judas and Mary:

- Mary is a woman. Judas is a man.
- Mary came to Jesus that night to anoint him with honor. Judas left and went to betray Jesus.
- Mary gave something extremely valuable to Jesus. Judas took a small amount of money to betray Jesus.
- Mary was generous. Judas became angry.
- Mary's act was beautiful. Judas's act was ugly.
- Mary was defended by Jesus. Judas was reprimanded by Jesus.

Mary knew Jesus was the resurrection and the life, and she understood he was going to the cross to die. Honoring her King with a burial anointing was not only a courageous act of vulnerability but also a smart move.

Part Three
Opening Our Minds

Another biblical example of a mindful woman of God that I hope we all aspire to emulate is Lydia from Acts 16. Lydia founded, funded, hosted, and led the first Christian church in Europe. She made history as the first person on the whole continent of Europe to put her faith in Christ.

On the apostle Paul's second major missionary trip, he met Lydia. He had set sail from Troas, a Greek city located in today's Turkey, with three of his buddies: Silas, Timothy, and Luke. When the four men arrived in Europe, their first stop was Philippi, where Lydia was living at the time. They stayed for a few days in the city and then on the Sabbath day, Saturday, the guys went outside the city gate by the river, where they thought there was a place of prayer.

Look up Acts 16:11–15.

➤ According to verses 14 and 15, what did Lydia do for a living?

➤ Where was she from?

A city girl through and through, Lydia hailed from a place called Thyatira (modern-day Turkey) that specialized in producing purple dye and purple cloth, which was a luxurious textile for the elite and nobles of the time. Think Hermès, Prada, Gucci.

At some point in the mid-first century, she moved from one urban area to another, migrating from Thyatira to Philippi, a Roman colony. We don't know why she moved or when.

But we do know her transition was good for business and that by the time we meet her in the Bible, she had been living there long enough to own a home.

Working in the trade of luxury goods, Lydia was a successful and independent business-woman and, as a result, wealthy. Although it's common for women to own homes in our day and age, it would have been unheard of in Lydia's culture. Apparently her home was large enough for her own family, potentially her employees, and room to spare to host the Philippian church and the four visiting preachers who shared the gospel with her. In addition, she had the economic means to bulk purchase her wares and ensure they transported from Thyatira, where they were made, to Philippi, where they were sold.

We don't know if Lydia was divorced or widowed when she got to Philippi, but some scholars assume she was a single mom with at least three or four children.[1] We see you, single moms! But it appears she was married at one time and was no longer married in Acts 16.

ACTS 16:14 NLT

As she listened to us, the Lord opened her heart, and she accepted what Paul was saying.

> How did the Lord open Lydia's heart?

> Who is the best listener you know and why?

Lydia's listening ears gave her an open mind. She accepted the new information Paul was giving to her about Jesus, and as a result, God changed her mind to know Christ as Savior. Lydia was an early adopter of the saving message of Jesus Christ, the first Christian on her continent.

Immortalized by God himself, what once seemed to me to be a hidden figure in church history was actually a leading lady refusing to let anything get in her way of knowing God. For some readers, the sheer fact that Lydia is in the Bible will make this a milestone moment in your life. It was for me. This savvy single mom and church-planting superwoman seemed to counterpunch all the things I was told about women from the Bible.

SIX

ALL YOUR STRENGTH

Group Time

Leader read Kat's message to the group:

As women, we rarely feel comfortable talking about our strengths. But the truth is God is all-powerful and he gives us his power through the Holy Spirit. If Jesus instructs all of us to love him with our strength, harnessing God's power to work through us is not only necessary; it's an act of surrender to God's priorities.

You and I might tend to think of power in relation to physical strength only, but the word is used 264 times in the Old Testament and the majority of the references mean spiritual strength. The strength of the Lord. Biblical language scholars of the New Testament define the Greek word for strength as "exceptional capability, with the probable implication of personal potential." They suggest translating the greatest commandment as, "Love the Lord your God as completely as you can."[1]

Consider the implications of reading the Great Commandment that way. It should cause us to serve God as completely as we can. In what ways has God made you exceptionally capable? Do you bring that to work and to your community of faith? Is there potential lying dormant in your life? A lost and dying world needs your contribution and it was put inside you for a great purpose.

Start with Prayer (2 minutes)

Have one person open in prayer. Ask God to reveal the ways he wants women to be strong in the Lord.

Scripture Reading (3 minutes)

Select volunteers to read the following passages:

PROVERBS 31:17–25 CSB

She draws on her strength
and reveals that her arms are strong.
She sees that her profits are good,
and her lamp never goes out at night.
She extends her hands to the spinning staff,
and her hands hold the spindle.
Her hands reach out to the poor,
and she extends her hands to the needy.
She is not afraid for her household when it snows,
for all in her household are doubly clothed.
She makes her own bed coverings;
her clothing is fine linen and purple.
Her husband is known at the city gates,
where he sits among the elders of the land.
She makes and sells linen garments;
she delivers belts to the merchants.
Strength and honor are her clothing,
and she can laugh at the time to come.

1 TIMOTHY 1:12 NLT

I thank Christ Jesus our Lord, who has given me strength to do his work. He considered me trustworthy and appointed me to serve him.

EPHESIANS 1:19–20 NLT

I also pray that you will understand the incredible greatness of God's power for us who believe him. This is the same mighty power that raised Christ from the dead and seated him in the place of honor at God's right hand in the heavenly realms.

1 PETER 4:10–11 CSB

Just as each one has received a gift, use it to serve others, as good managers of the varied grace of God. If anyone speaks, it should be as one who speaks God's words; if anyone serves, it should be from the strength God provides, so that God may be glorified through Jesus Christ in everything.

Watch Session 6 Video (15 minutes)

Video Notes

Jesus has given you the strength to do his work.

We were designed to be warrior-strong, and we should own it.

Somewhere along the way, we started to believe women are not supposed to be powerful.

If we love God with all our strength we are going to become strong women of God through God's power.

According to a 2018 Pew Research study, "Americans are much more likely to use *powerful* in a positive way to describe men than women."

"Too strong" is not a thing for Jesus women.

Group Discussion (35 minutes)

Based on the Proverbs 31:17–25 Scripture reading:

➤ What is the Proverbs 31 woman able to accomplish because she is strong?

➤ Verse 25 contains figurative language about this strong woman of God. She is "clothed with strength and honor." What do you think it means to be clothed with strength?

Based on the 1 Timothy 1:12 Scripture reading:

➤ Why does God give us strength?

➤ What work has God called you to do?

Based on the Ephesians 1:19–20 Scripture reading:

➤ What kind of power does God give us?

➤ Where have you heard that women can be "too strong?"

Based on the 1 Peter 4:10–11 Scripture reading:

➤ What does Peter tell us we must do with the gifts we receive from God?

➤ How does God distribute his gifts to us?

➤ How should these truths change our lives?

➤ What is holding you back from growing in strength?

End in Prayer (5 minutes)

Use the prayer cards in the back of this study guide to share prayer requests. Choose one person to close your time together in prayer, asking God to help you love him with all your strength.

Suggested Reading in
No More Holding Back:

Chapter 9

Session Six

ALL YOUR STRENGTH
PERSONAL STUDY

Part One
Multiply and Rule

According to the creation account in Genesis, God created women to be helpers. Like it or not, that's the truth. But not the kind of help an administrative assistant gives to the boss, a babysitter provides to an overwhelmed momma, or the oppressive form African American women experienced serving in white households as seen in *The Help*. No. Even leading ladies fit the supporting roles God has designed for us. I promise. The question is, what kind of support does God have in mind for women? 'Cause nobody puts Baby in the corner.

Biblical womanhood's archetype is Eve, the first woman created by God from Adam's rib.

Read Genesis 1:26–31 and 2:1–25.

➤ Why did God create Eve? (Genesis 2:18)

God's solution was to make a helper "suitable for him." What I wanted to know was what did Adam need help with in Eden, and what does *suitable* mean?

Indebted to Carolyn Custis James, I bring you some of the points she made in her life-changing book *When Life and Beliefs Collide*. Did Adam need a domestic engineer, someone to manage the house? No, he didn't. No houses needed keeping in the garden of Eden. Did Adam need someone to cook? Nope, they ate from the garden produce. Did he need someone to help with laundry? Again, no. They were naked. What about the kids—did Adam need someone to raise the kids? At this time, they had no children to rear. Did he only need a companion to alleviate his aloneness? Nope. He was in the presence of God, where all fullness of joy can be found (Psalm 16:11).[1]

While Adam did not require assistance managing a house, cooking, cleaning, doing laundry, raising children, or companionship, all those essential responsibilities must get done in modern households. In my own family, most of these weekly tasks fall to me. Yet while my contributions to our family are priceless, they do not comprise a woman's truest purpose on earth. I would go so far to say that it doesn't matter how the obligations of "adulting" are delegated as long as they get done.

Furthermore, marriage was not Eve's greatest joy, and raising a family was not her highest calling, because helping is not limited to being a wife and a mother. We can maintain that both roles are beautiful expressions of someone who is helpful, while recognizing that they are not the definition of a helper.

Adam's placement in the garden happened before Eve was even fashioned. The sequence of events matters, because it speaks to the purpose of all women and men.

➤ What did God assign to Adam as his work? (Genesis 2:15)

That's what Adam needed help with, a partner to nurture the earth.

➤ What did God tell both Adam and Eve to do in Genesis 1:28?

Could it be that in addition to gendering the Great Commandment we have done the same with the Cultural Mandate in Genesis 1:28? Have we made *multiplying* women's work and *ruling* men's work? Listen closely, people of the Book: the preeminent role of any woman (and man) is multiplying *and* ruling.

But don't let the word *multiplying* throw you. One might assume that Eve and Adam's responsibility of multiplying is limited to procreation, but the problem with this is Jesus.

➤ What does Colossians 1:15 say about Jesus?

Whatever God appointed Adam and Eve to do, Jesus accomplished the same—flawlessly. Jesus fulfills all of God's tasks and orders, yet he was single with no biological children. So, how did Jesus fulfill the mandate to be fruitful and multiply, to fill the earth? Jesus produced disciples.

➤ What does Jesus commission all his disciples to do in Matthew 28:19?

To all the women passing on their faith to their friends, coworkers, family members, children, and loved ones, keep at it. Making disciples is our thing.

I wonder what kind of tidal wave of revival would break out if we took to heart God's words in the garden. Do we assign more value to a woman's calling to multiply than we do to rule? Do we assign more value to a man's calling to rule than we do to multiply?

What I know for sure, is that we all need God's strength to multiply and rule the way he intended.

➤ If women are equally created to rule the earth and reproduce Christ-followers alongside men, does that change the way you approach life?

Part Two
Helpful Helpers

Per usual, the Bible has persuaded me and changed me in the process. Originally designed to guard the garden, I have found a new purpose in life: to rule and multiply with my brothers in Christ as a warrior-helper. That much makes sense to me. But how? What is the best way to help?

Baffling his disciples, Jesus used a teachable moment to contrast the helper roles in God's kingdom against the leadership roles of the world that require a pecking order.

Read Matthew 20:20–28.

➤ According to verses 25–28, what did Jesus come to do?

➤ What did he not come to do?

Dominant, charismatic leaders naturally draw followers looking for direction. There is something to be said for the ones at the top helping us find our way. But once we learn the ways of Jesus and the rhythms of his kingdom, we will follow his lead—bowing low, with our knees on the earth, to wash people's feet. Maybe we've made too much of certain personality types or leadership skills. It's time to welcome every human into a posture of humility.

Being a good helper will mean emulating God himself, since he is the supreme Helper.

Read Psalm 146.

> List at least 9 ways God is helpful in Psalm 146:5–10.

1. _____
2. _____
3. _____
4. _____
5. _____
6. _____
7. _____
8. _____
9. _____

The passage above is clear: helpers uphold the cause of the oppressed and give food to the hungry. Helpers set the prisoners free, give sight to the blind, lift up those who are bowed down, and love the righteous. Helpers watch over the foreigner, sustain the fatherless and the widow, and frustrate the ways of the wicked. Helpers reign.

Let's be the kind of women known for our character. When people talk about us, may they say that we protect people who need an advocate, that we are a stronghold and a shield to those who need a buffer from pain and suffering. When people talk about us, may they say we are always sticking up for people, speaking up for the voiceless, staying strong for the powerless. In the marketplace we champion our coworkers, at home we uphold the people we love, in society we build up . . . everyone.

As far as it's up to us, let's be women who fearlessly welcome refugees, generously meet the needs of the vulnerable, and confuse our enemies with kindness. When our names pop into someone's head, let's be known as the ones you can always count on for a helping hand. Helpers: This. Is. Us.

The outcast and the outsiders are *our* people. If you mess with the marginalized, you mess with us, the warrior-women fashioned to reign. The Enemy will have to go through us before hijacking the next generation. Forces of darkness will face us on the battlefield when the gospel work gets dangerous. And we are up for the challenge because we are the daughters of the church.

Part Three
Strong Helpers

You did it! This is the final lesson in the study guide. And it happens to be my favorite part of the whole study. It's a tad longer than usual. But it's worth it.

Does God make mistakes? I don't think I'm not as feminine as I think I am supposed to be. Maybe the God of the universe was napping when I was formed in my mother's womb. These thoughts kept running through my head before Carolyn Custis James's research introduced me to the Hebrew word *ezer* (pronounced "ay-zer"), which is usually translated "helper" in the Old Testament. Ms. James suggests that the word *helper* in Genesis would best be translated "warrior" because, "Scholars tallied up the twenty-one times *ezer* appears in the Old Testament: twice in Genesis for the woman, three times for nations to whom Israel appealed for military aid, and—here's the kicker—sixteen times for God as Israel's helper."[2] The point is, God was protecting them like a warrior in battle. See for yourself.

➤ Circle the word **helper** (the Hebrew word *ezer*) in each of the twenty-one Old Testament references that follow, and then answer the "helper/helping" questions as a group activity:

GENESIS 2:18 NASB

Then the Lord God said, "It is not good for the man to be alone; I will make him a helper suitable for him."

➤ Who is the helper?

➤ How are they helping?

GENESIS 2:20 NASB

The man gave names to all the cattle, and to the birds of the sky, and to every beast of the field, but for Adam there was not found a helper suitable for him.

➤ Who is the helper?

➤ How are they helping?

EXODUS 18:4 NASB

The other was named Eliezer, for he said, "The God of my father was my help, and delivered me from the sword of Pharaoh."

Moses envisioned God delivering the Israelites from the sword of Pharaoh when he named his son Eliezer, which means "God is my help."

➤ Who is the helper?

➤ How are they helping?

DEUTERONOMY 33:7 NASB

Hear, O Lord, the voice of Judah, and bring him to his people. With his hands he contended for them, and may You be a help against his adversaries.

As Moses prayed for Judah, he asked God to hear his prayers and be Judah's help against his adversaries, because the tribe of Judah marched as the head of the tribes, the literal front line of every battle.

> Who is the helper?

> How are they helping?

DEUTERONOMY 33:26 NASB

There is none like the God of Jeshurun, who rides the heavens to your help, and through the skies in His majesty.

Moses prayed for Asher while ascribing to God his glory. There is no one like God, Moses said, for he rides the heavens to help us. In no uncertain terms, his prayer was about Asher crushing it in life because of the security God afforded him.

> Who is the helper?

➤ How are they helping?

DEUTERONOMY 33:29 NASB

Blessed are you, O Israel; who is like you, a people saved by the LORD, who is the shield of your help and the sword of your majesty! So your enemies will cringe before you, and you will tread upon their high places.

Moses told all Israel that they would be blessed because the Lord is a shield of protection and a sword of majesty.

➤ Who is the helper?

➤ How are they helping?

PSALM 20:2 NASB

May He send you help from the sanctuary and support you from Zion!

The author of this psalm used the word *help* to say, "God's help sustains us."

➤ Who is the helper?

➤ How are they helping?

PSALM 33:20 NASB

Our soul waits for the LORD; He is our help and our shield.

➤ Who is the helper?

➤ How are they helping?

PSALM 70:5 NASB

I am afflicted and needy; hasten to me, O God! You are my help and my deliverer;
O LORD, do not delay.

➤ Who is the helper?

➤ How are they helping?

PSALM 89:19 NASB

Once You spoke in vision to Your godly ones, and said, "I have given help to
one who is mighty; I have exalted one chosen from the people."

➤ Who is the helper?

➤ How are they helping?

PSALM 115:9 NASB

O Israel, trust in the LORD; He is their help and their shield.

Unlike the nations worshiping silver and gold idols made by human hands, the Israelites worshiped Yahweh.

➤ Who is the helper?

➤ How are they helping?

PSALM 115:10 NASB

O house of Aaron, trust in the LORD; He is their help and their shield.

➤ Who is the helper?

➤ How are they helping?

PSALM 115:11 NASB

You who fear the LORD, trust in the LORD; He is their help and their shield.

➤ Who is the helper?

➤ How are they helping?

PSALM 121:1 NASB

I will lift up my eyes to the mountains; from where shall my help come?

This verse should sound familiar to some who might sing a similar song on Sunday morning at church. Singing a processional song of ascent on the annual journey to Jerusalem, God's people sang that the Lord was on their side.

➤ Who is the helper?

➤ How are they helping?

PSALM 121:2 NASB

My help comes from the LORD, who made heaven and earth.

This is the second verse in that song of ascent, and later in the same psalm the author said if God was not their helper they would be attacked and swallowed alive, the waters of the Nile engulfing them with raging waters.

> Who is the helper?

> How are they helping?

PSALM 124:8 NASB

Our help is in the name of the LORD, who made heaven and earth.

The thread weaving these hymns together is the word *ezer*, which is used every time to describe God's helping hand in battle.

> Who is the helper?

> How are they helping?

PSALM 146:5 NASB

How blessed is he whose help is the God of Jacob, whose hope is in the LORD his God.

➤ Who is the helper?

➤ How are they helping?

ISAIAH 30:5 NASB

Everyone will be ashamed because of a people who cannot profit them, who are not for help or profit, but for shame and also for reproach.

The use of the word *help* in this verse and the next two refer to nations to whom Israel appealed for military aid.

➤ Who is the helper?

➤ How are they helping?

EZEKIEL 12:14 NASB

I will scatter to every wind all who are around him, his helpers and all his troops; and I will draw out a sword after them.

➤ Who is the helper?

➤ How are they helping?

DANIEL 11:34 NASB

Now when they fall they will be granted a little help, and many will join with them in hypocrisy.

➤ Who is the helper?

➤ How are they helping?

HOSEA 13:9 NASB

It is your destruction, O Israel, that you are against Me, against your help.

This is God's indictment through the prophet Hosea of any Israelite resisting God's help.

➤ Who is the helper?

➤ How are they helping?

God designed women to be helpers but not the kind of help Robin gives to Batman or an associate gives to the boss. No. We were imaged after God himself and given the ability to help the way he does, by fighting and winning battles, holding nothing back from our devotion to Christ.

LEADER'S GUIDE

After washing their feet, he put on his robe again and sat down and asked, "Do you understand what I was doing? You call me 'Teacher' and 'Lord,' and you are right, because that's what I am. And since I, your Lord and Teacher, have washed your feet, you ought to wash each other's feet. I have given you an example to follow. Do as I have done to you."

John 13:12–15 NLT

You are brave. Leading a group is a simple but profound act of service to the women in your group, and I for one am really proud of your willingness to model Jesus' brand of leadership. The kind that bends low to serve. In my experience, leading a group not only encourages the women around you, but it also serves as a way to be more connected to Christ, more in tune with his Spirit and more in love with the Scriptures.

Start with Prayer

I've led countless small groups through Bible study curriculum and the most meaningful groups have been the ones covered in prayer. Take some time now to commit your group to God. Invite the Holy Spirit to counsel, teach, and comfort everyone in your group.

Brainstorm

➤ Where should you host this group?

➤ Who should you invite?

1. _____   5. _____
2. _____   6. _____
3. _____   7. _____
4. _____   8. _____

➤ Which leader at your church could help support you as you lead the group?

➤ Which licensed professional counselors could you refer your group members to when they need professional care?

Cultivate Ownership

Each of the most tight-knit groups I have led have had something in common: we cultivated ownership. Everyone felt like the group was *their* group. Here are several ways you could involve the women in your group to participate and prepare them to lead future groups themselves:

- If you notice a future leader holding back from the conversation, call on her by name and ask her thoughts on the topic.
- If you know someone's personal story would be valuable insight into a topic that comes up in the study, ask her before you meet as a group if she would be willing to bring up her own experiences in that area. This way she won't feel like she is on the spot.
- Ask different women in the group to open and close in prayer.
- Prepare in advance who you will ask to read the Scripture readings in each group discussion.

APPENDIX

LOVING YOUR COMMUNITY WELL

Dr. Kay Daigle, *Beyond Ordinary Women*

➤ Come prepared, even thinking in advance of what was most meaningful to you from the study guide so that you can share it with the group.

➤ Be on time, in fact plan to be early, so you aren't a distraction.

➤ Please participate. God has you here, and you never know how he will use what you say in someone else's life.

➤ Don't talk on every question. Instead, be thoughtful, allowing others to answer. If you discuss one question, be quiet and listen to several more before answering again. Ask God to nudge you when you need to speak.

➤ Listen well to the others in your group and ask God to help you learn from them about him. Ask him to give you insights into how to support and love them well.

➤ Stay on topic. Good conversations are fun, but leave them until the discussion is over. Practice listening and holding your thoughts until the appropriate time.

➤ Don't discuss politics, even in an election year. This time is about God, not the political situation. In an election year this may be difficult, but please realize that not everyone thinks as you do, and we want every woman to feel loved and welcomed, as Jesus himself would do. Of course, the Bible deals with issues, but keep the conversation biblical rather than bringing up parties or politicians.

➤ Do not speak negatively of other churches or denominations. You can mention one positively, and you can let everyone know where you go to church. When you share about your past, if it includes a negative experience in a church, please do not name the church or denomination to be sensitive to the group.

➤ Don't try to fix the problems of others group members. If someone shares an issue or difficulty, support her with kind encouraging words or pray for her. Know that God is there to help. He knows best what she should do.

➤ Be patient with those in your group. We are all in different places in our walks with God. Give the same grace to others to develop and grow that you want from them.

SESSION 2 GROUP ACTIVITY ANSWERS

(See page 22.)

Eve (Genesis 2–3)	Mary Magdalene (John 20:1–18)
Eve is in the Garden of **Eden**	Mary is in the garden **tomb**
Eve is placed inside the Garden by **God**	Mary comes to the garden by her own initiative
Eve was forbidden to eat the fruit during the day	Mary comes to the tomb when it is still **dark** outside
Eve was created after Adam	Mary is the **first** person to see Jesus risen from the dead—before Peter, before John
Eve faced the fruit-producing tree of **life**	Mary faced a tomb of **death**
Eve initiated a curse of **death** for all people with her rebellion	Mary initiated the resurrection **life** for all people with her obedience
The Serpent approached Eve with cunning questions that sowed doubt	Angels greeted Mary and then Jesus himself appeared to her, and they asked compassionate questions that sowed hope
Eve hid her **naked** shame from God's presence before she was ousted from Eden	Mary wept without shame in Jesus' presence, and it was Jesus' cloths that were missing
Eve was **deceived**	Mary was commissioned
Eve rebelled	Mary obeyed

PRAYER CARDS

Each week use one of these cards to share prayer requests. Write your name and request on one card and pass it to someone in the group. Commit to pray for one person in your group in between your group meetings.

ENDNOTES

Session 2 Personal Study

1. Ron Pierce, "Deborah: Only When a Good Man Is Hard to Find?" Sandra Glahn, ed., *Vindicating the Vixens: Revisiting Sexualized, Vilified, and Marginalized Women of the Bible* (Grand Rapids, MI: Kregel, 2017), 195–96. "12:41–42: There were 13 trumpet-shaped receptacles (Heb. *shofar*) that the priests had placed against the north, east, and south walls of the women's courtyard to receive the Jews' offerings. 644: The court of the women (temple's "treasury") was within the court of the Gentiles, the outermost court of the temple. A low barrier separated the court of the Gentiles from the other courtyards and the temple building that lay within this enclosure. The court of the women was farther from the temple building than the court of Israel, which only Jewish men could enter, or the court of the priests, which only the priests could enter. Jesus had given His preceding teaching in the court of the Gentiles. Now He evidently moved into the court of the women. 643: See Geoffrey Smith, "A Closer Look at the Widow's Offering: Mark 12:41–44," *Journal of the Evangelical Theological Society* 40:1 (March 1997) 27–36. 644: *Mishnah Shekalim* 6:5. See also Alfred Edersheim, *The Temple*, 48–49.
2. Dr. Thomas L. Constable, *Expository Bible Study Notes*, "Mark," http://planobiblechapel.org/tcon/notes/pdf/mark.pdf, 184.
3. J. R. Edwards, *The Gospel According to Mark* (Grand Rapids, MI: Eerdmans, 2002), 381.

Session 3 Personal Study

1. F. L Cross and E. A. Livingstone, eds., *The Oxford Dictionary of the Christian Church*, 3rd ed. rev. (New York: Oxford University Press, 2005), 744.

Session 4: All Your Soul

1. C. Schultz, "Soul," *Evangelical Dictionary of Biblical Theology*, electronic ed. (Grand Rapids, MI: Baker, 1996), 743–44.
2. E. E. Carpenter and P. W. Comfort, *Holman Treasury of Key Bible Words: 200 Greek and 200 Hebrew Words Defined and Explained* (Nashville: Broadman and Holman Publishers, 2000), 178.

Session 4 Personal Study

1. Timothy Ralston, PhD, "Ch. 5: The Virgin Mary: Reclaiming Our Respect," Sandra Glahn, ed., *Vindicating the Vixens: Revisiting Sexualized, Vilified, and Marginalized Women of the Bible* (Grand Rapids, MI: Kregel, 2017), 102.

Session 5 Personal Study

1. *Vindicating the Vixens*, 45.

Session 6: All Your Strength

1. J. P. Louw and E. A. Nida, *Greek-English Lexicon of the New Testament: Based on Semantic Domains* (electronic ed. of the 2nd edition., vol. 1, p. 675). New York: United Bible Societies, 1996.

Session 6 Personal Study

1. Carolyn Custis James, *When Life and Beliefs Collide* (Grand Rapids, MI: Zondervan, 2002), 180ff.
2. James, *Half the Church* (Grand Rapids, MI: Zondervan, 2016), 112.

ABOUT THE AUTHOR

Kat Armstrong has been encouraging women to love God and others with their all for almost 20 years as a Bible teacher. Kat holds a Master of Christian Education from Dallas Theological Seminary and is the cofounder of Polished, a network to gather young professional women to navigate career and explore faith together, and the host of the Polished Podcast. Her husband is the pastor of Dallas Bible Church and she has a six-year-old son.

www.polishedonline.org
@polished.online

POLISHED

A network to gather young professional women to navigate career and explore faith together.

Start a chapter in your city for local events

⟶ polishedonline.org/startachapter

Join the online network for discounted ticket prices, digital downloads, and access to our online community

⟶ polishedonline.org/network

Listen to the Polished Podcast

⟶ polishedonline.org/podcast

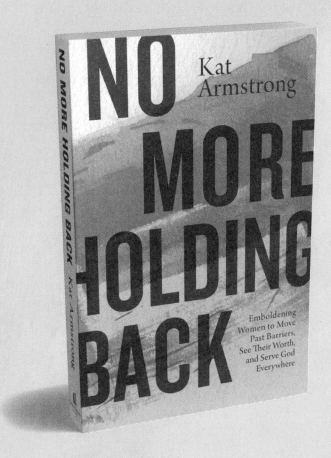